THE OFFICIAL
QUEEN PARK RANGERS
FOOTBALL CLUB
QUIZ BOOK

THE OFFICIAL QUEENS PARK RANGERS FOOTBALL CLUB QUIZ BOOK

Compiled by
Chris Cowlin and Kevin Snelgrove

Foreword by Neil Warnock

APEX PUBLISHING LTD

Hardback first published in 2010 by
Apex Publishing Ltd
PO Box 7086, Clacton on Sea, Essex, CO15 5WN, England
www.apexpublishing.co.uk

Copyright © 2010 by Chris Cowlin and Kevin Snelgrove
The authors have asserted their moral rights

British Library Cataloguing-in-Publication Data
A catalogue record for this book
is available from the British Library

ISBN HARDBACK: 1-906358-92-3   978-1-906358-92-1

Typeset in 10.5pt Chianti Bdlt Win95BT

Cover Design: Siobhan Smith

Printed in Great Britain by the
MPG Books Group, Bodmin and King's Lynn

Author's Note:
Please can you contact me: **ChrisCowlin@btconnect.com** if you find any mistakes/errors in this book as I would like to put them right on any future reprints of this book. I would also like to hear from Queens Park Rangers fans who have enjoyed the test! For more information on me and my books please look at: **www.ChrisCowlin.com**

This book is an official product of Queens Park Rangers Football Club

We would like to dedicate this book to:

All the players and staff who have worked for the club during their history.

FOREWORD

I am very honoured to write the foreword to the first ever quiz book published on Queens Park Rangers Football Club.

As you will know I arrived at Loftus Road as club manager at the start of March 2010. I first took charge of The Super-Hoops in an emphatic 3-1 home win against West Bromwich Albion, it was nice to get a winning start in my QPR managerial career. And on a personal note it was wonderful to receive the manager of the month award in the Championship for August and September 2010 as the team were doing so well.

The history of Queens Park Rangers Football Club is long and varied and I'm sure the questions in this book will bring back plenty of memories. As we continue to write new chapters in the club's history it's always fitting to remember what went before.

This super quiz book is a must for all Rangers fans, regardless of age, I have seen other books compiled by Chris and Kevin, and they are very good in testing the fans knowledge of the club and its players and finding fascinating facts, which will help fans to learn more about their club. I was just glad I got 10 out of 10 on the Neil Warnock section!

Best wishes

Neil Warnock

INTRODUCTION

I would first of all like to thank Neil Warnock for writing the foreword to this book. I am very grateful for his help on this project.

I would also like to thank all the people who have provided a comment and/or review on this book.

I would also like to thank Francis Atkinson at Queens Park Rangers Football Club for all his help during the books production.

I hope you enjoy this book. Hopefully it should bring back some wonderful memories!

It was great working with Kevin Snelgrove again, between us I hope we have given you a selection of easy, medium and hard questions.

In closing, I would like to thank all my friends and family for encouraging me to complete this book.

Best wishes
Chris Cowlin

www.apexpublishing.co.uk

CLUB HISTORY

1. In what year was Queens Park Rangers founded?

2. What is the name of Queens Park Rangers' stadium?

3. Who was manager of Queens Park Rangers from April 1944 to May 1952?

4. What are Queens Park Rangers' three nicknames?

5. Which team were Queens Park Rangers first League opponents on 9 September 1899, a game they lost 1-0?

6. In March 1967 Queens Park Rangers became the first Third Division club to win the League Cup. Which team did they beat 3-2 in the final at Wembley?

7. What is the capacity of Queens Park Rangers' stadium – 18,100, 19,100 or 20,100?

8. In 1979 which teenager did Queens Park Rangers sell to Arsenal for £1 million?

9. In the 1984/85 UEFA Cup Queens Park Rangers beat which team 6-2 at home and then suffered a 4-0 defeat in the away leg, going out on the away goals rule?

10. Which manager took charge of Queens Park Rangers in March 2010?

2010/2011

11. Can you name the defender who wore squad number 3 during this season?

12. Which striker did QPR sign from Portsmouth on 31 August 2010?

13. Which club did QPR beat 4-0 at home on the opening day of the League season?

14. Which East Anglian club did Rangers beat 3-0 away from home during September 2010?

15. Following on from the previous question, which forward scored a brace in the game?

16. Which Latvian defender scored a brace for QPR in their 3-0 home win over Doncaster Rovers during September 2010?

17. True or false: QPR were unbeaten in the League during August 2010, in their first four League matches of the season?

18. What was the score when Millwall visited Loftus Road during September 2010?

19. Which forward signed for QPR from Derby County on 31 August 2010?

20. Which Moroccan midfielder signed for QPR from Tottenham in August 2010, having already had two loan spells at Loftus Road?

CLUB HONOURS

Match up the year with the Queens Park Rangers honour

21.	Division Two Champions	1967
22.	Division Three Champions	1986
23.	Southern League Champions	1967
24.	Division Three South Champions	1895
25.	FA Cup Runners-Up	1906
26.	London Cup Winners	1976
27.	League Cup Winners	1982
28.	Western League Champions	1948
29.	League Cup Runners-Up	1912
30.	Division One Runners-Up	1983

TONY INGHAM

31. True or false: a function room at Loftus Road was named in Tony's honour?

32. How many League appearances did Tony make for The R's in his career – 504, 514 or 524?

33. What position did Tony take at Loftus Road in 1981?

34. From which Yorkshire team did Tony sign for QPR, having made only three League appearances for them?

35. True or false: Tony holds a club record for making 272 successive League and Cup appearances for QPR, including five seasons as an ever-present player?

36. How many League goals did Tony score for QPR in his career – 3, 13 or 23?

37. Against which club did Tony make his QPR League debut during November 1950 – Doncaster Rovers, Sheffield United or Sheffield Wednesday?

38. In which position did Tony play during his playing days – defender, midfielder or striker?

39. In which year was Tony born in Harrogate – 1924, 1925 or 1926?

40. True or false: Tony won three international caps for England during his football playing career?

WHERE DID THEY GO? – 1

Match up the player with the club he joined
when he left Queens Park Rangers

41.	Leighton James	Arsenal
42.	Ian Holloway	Coventry City
43.	Gary Penrice	Blackburn Rovers
44.	David Webb	Watford
45.	Kenny Sansom	Blackpool
46.	Trevor Francis	Leicester City
47.	David Bardsley	Burnley
48.	John Hollins	Nottingham Forest
49.	Nigel Quashie (first spell)	Sheffield Wednesday
50.	Roy Wegerle	Bristol Rovers

GEORGE GODDARD

51. In what position did George play during his playing days?

52. How many League goals did George score for QPR in his playing career – 173, 177 or 181?

53. True or false: George holds a club record for scoring the most League goals in QPR's history?

54. In which year did George sign for Queens Park Rangers – 1924, 1925 or 1926?

55. From which club did George sign when he joined The R's?

56. In which year was George born in Surrey - 1903, 1906 or 1909?

57. True or false: George once had a playing spell at Southend United?

58. Why did George leave QPR in 1933 – the club needed the money, George had an argument with his manager or George moved house and needed to be closer to his family?

59. For which club did George sign when he left QPR in December 1933?

60. How many League goals did George score for The R's during the 1929/30 season, a club record?

MANAGERS – 1

*Match up the manager with the time he was
in charge at Queens Park Rangers*

61.	Ian Holloway	1985-88
62.	James Cowan	1980-84
63.	Gordon Jago	1907-13
64.	Terry Venables	1952-59
65.	Alec Stock	1989-91
66.	Ray Wilkins	1971-74
67.	Jack Taylor	1998-2001
68.	Don Howe	2001-06
69.	Gerry Francis (second spell)	1959-68
70.	Jim Smith	1994-96

2009/2010

71. Which team did QPR beat 2-1 at Loftus Road on Boxing Day 2009?

72. Which London club did The R's beat 2-0 away from home during April 2010, with Ákos Buzsáky and Kaspars Gorkšs scoring the goals?

73. How many of their 46 League games did QPR win - 14, 16 or 18?

74. With which team did QPR share a 1-1 home draw on the opening day of the League season?

75. Which midfielder scored the only goal in the club's 1-0 away win at Barnsley in the League during April 2010?

76. What was the score when QPR visited Pride Park and played Derby County during October 2009 in the League?

77. Can you name the two goalkeepers that played in QPR's 46 League matches during this season?

78. Which striker finished as the club's highest League scorer with 12 goals during this season?

79. Which midfielder did QPR sell to Newcastle United during January 2010?

80. In what position in the Championship did The R's finish this season?

NATIONALITIES – 1

Match up the player with his nationality

81. Danny Shittu	*Latvian*
82. Roy Wegerle	*Dutch*
83. Gino Padula	*Nigerian*
84. Kaspars Gorkšs	*French*
85. Luděk Mikloško	*English*
86. Adel Taarabt	*American*
87. Georges Santos	*Czechoslovakian*
88. Ned Zelić	*Moroccan*
89. Chris Kiwomya	*Australian*
90. Sieb Dijkstra	*Argentinian*

2008/2009

91. How many of their 46 League matches did QPR win – 15, 17 or 19?

92. Who started this season as The R's boss, only to leave in October 2008?

93. Which Iceland forward signed for QPR in January 2009, after a loan spell from Bolton from November 2008 until January 2009?

94. Which team did QPR beat 3-0 away from home in the League during January 2009, with Heidar Helguson scoring a brace?

95. In which position did QPR finish in the Championship – 9th, 10th or 11th?

96. How many League goals did Dexter Blackstock score for QPR, finishing as the club's highest scorer for this season?

97. True or false: QPR were unbeaten in their five League matches during October 2008?

98. Which team did QPR beat 3-2 at home in the League during April 2009, having been 2-0 down after 53 minutes, with Damion Stewart scoring the winning 88th-minute goal?

99. Which R's striker scored a brace in a 4-1 home League win against Southampton during September 2008?

100. With which London team did QPR share a 2-2 away League draw on Boxing Day 2008?

WHERE DID THEY COME FROM? – 1

*Match up the player with the club he left
to join Queens Park Rangers*

101.	Tony Currie	Notts County
102.	Ákos Buzsáky	Arsenal
103.	Roy Faulkner	Leeds United
104.	Frank McLintock	Rangers
105.	Don Masson	Brentford
106.	Fitz Hall	Plymouth Argyle
107.	Martin Rowlands	Crystal Palace
108.	Vinnie Jones	Wigan Athletic
109.	Mark Hateley	Blackburn Rovers
110.	Clive Allen (second spell)	Wimbledon

2007/2008

111. Which team did QPR beat 3-1 at Loftus Road on New Year's Day 2008?

112. Which midfielder scored a brace in The R's 3-0 home League win against Stoke City during March 2008?

113. With which club did QPR share a 2-2 away draw on the opening day of this League season?

114. Who was the only R's player to play in all 46 League matches during this season?

115. How many League goals did Rowan Vine score for QPR during this season – 6, 7 or 8?

116. Which defender did QPR sign from Wigan Athletic during January 2008?

117. Which forward scored a brace in QPR's 3-2 away League win at Southampton during February 2008?

118. Which team did QPR beat 1-0 at home during October 2007, with Martin Rowlands scoring the only goal from the penalty spot in the 67th minute?

119. How many of their 46 League games did QPR win – 14, 15 or 16?

120. Which midfielder left Loftus Road for Gillingham during August 2007?

POSITIONS IN THE LEAGUE – 1

*Match up the season/points with the club's
finishing position in the League*

121.	1971/72, 54 points	8th
122.	1991/92, 54 points	23rd
123.	1949/50, 34 points	4th
124.	1957/58, 50 points	21st
125.	1979/80, 49 points	1st
126.	1982/83, 85 points	20th
127.	1913/14, 41 points	10th
128.	1928/29, 52 points	11th
129.	2005/06, 50 points	6th
130.	2000/01, 40 points	5th

131. *In which position did the club finish in the Championship – 18th, 19th or 20th?*

132. *What was the average attendance at Loftus Road during this season – 10,936, 11,936 or 12,936?*

133. *Which striker wore the squad number 29 during this season?*

134. *Which Irish midfielder finished the season with 10 League goals during this season?*

135. *Which midfielder did QPR sign from Derby County during January 2007?*

136. *Which Nigerian defender left Loftus Road in August 2006 for Watford?*

137. *Which Hoops striker scored 13 League goals, finishing the season as the club's highest scorer?*

138. *Which former player took charge at Loftus Road during September 2006?*

139. *True or false: QPR won only one of their first eight League matches during this season?*

140. *How many of their 46 League matches did the club win during this season - 14, 15 or 16?*

POSITIONS IN THE LEAGUE – 2

Match up the season/points with the club's finishing position in the League

141.	2002/03, 83 points		12th
142.	1988/89, 53 points		22nd
143.	1966/67, 67 points		9th
144.	1995/96, 33 points		2nd
145.	1975/76, 59 points		11th
146.	1932/33, 37 points		1st
147.	1901/02, 23 points		15th
148.	2004/05, 62 points		16th
149.	1968/69, 18 points		4th
150.	1954/55, 44 points		19th

LEAGUE CUP RUNNERS-UP
1985/1986

151. Which team did QPR beat 3-2 over two legs in the semi-finals?

152. Which London club did The R's knock out in the League Cup quarter-finals, winning 2-0 in the replay away from home?

153. Which team beat QPR 3-0 in the final?

154. Which QPR manager guided the club to the League Cup final?

155. Who played in goal for QPR in the League Cup final?

156. Can you name the two Irish players who played for The R's in the final?

157. In which month of 1986 was the final played?

158. Which team did The R's beat 3-1 at home in the 4th round?

159. What was the League Cup known as during this year – Carling Cup, Milk Cup or Worthington Cup?

160. Which team did QPR beat 3-0 at home in the 1st leg and 5-1 away in the 2nd leg in the 2nd round of the competition, played in September and October 1985?

SQUAD NUMBERS 2010/2011 - 1

Match the player with their squad number

161.	Fitz Hall	14
162.	Jamie Mackie	1
163.	Paddy Kenny	22
164.	Rob Hulse	5
165.	Adel Taarabt	10
166.	Martin Rowlands	12
167.	Clint Hill	8
168.	Peter Ramage	3
169.	Ákos Buzsáky	7
170.	Leon Clarke	20

LES FERDINAND

171. Against which team did Les make his R's debut, in a
4-0 away defeat in April 1987?

172. How many League goals did Les score for QPR during
the 1994/95 Premier League season – 22, 24 or 26?

173. For which team did Les sign when he left Loftus Road
in June 1995?

174. True or false: Les was awarded an MBE in the 2005
Queen's Birthday Honours List?

175. From which club did QPR sign Les in 1987?

176. How many goals did Les score for England in his 17 full
international caps?

177. What was Les's nickname?

178. In what position did Les play during his playing days?

179. In which year was Les born in Acton, London – 1964,
1965 or 1966?

180. How many League goals did Les score for QPR in his
football career – 70, 80 or 90?

WHERE DID THEY GO? – 2

*Match up the player with the club he joined
when he left Queens Park Rangers*

181.	Steve Hodge	Rangers
182.	Clive Walker	Portsmouth
183.	Dean Sturridge	West Ham United
184.	Dennis Oli	Bristol Rovers
185.	Andy Impey	Newcastle United
186.	Nigel Spackman	Watford
187.	Glenn Roeder	Kidderminster Harriers
188.	Andy Tillson	Leicester City
189.	Eddie Kelly	Swansea City
190.	Ernie Howe	Fulham

TREVOR SINCLAIR

191. From which club did Trevor sign when he arrived at Loftus Road in 1993?

192. What is Trevor's middle name – Lloyd, Lewis or Leonard?

193. True or false: Trevor won the Premier League Player of the Month award for October 1995?

194. How many full international caps did Trevor win for his country?

195. Against which club did Trevor score his first League goal for QPR, in a 2-1 home win during September 1993?

196. How many League goals did Trevor score for The R's during his first season at the club, 1993/94?

197. Against which team did Trevor score a QPR brace in a 2-1 home League win during August 1997?

198. How much did Trevor cost QPR when the club purchased him in August 1993?

199. What squad number did Trevor wear during the 1993/94, 1994/95 and 1995/96 seasons in the Premier League?

200. For which London club did Trevor sign when he left QPR in January 1998?

MANAGERS – 2

Match up the manager with the time he was in charge at Queens Park Rangers

201. Dave Sexton	1997-98
202. Gerry Francis (first spell)	1925-31
203. Robert Hewison	1988-89
204. John Gregory	1913-20
205. Billy Birrell	1977-78
206. James Howie	2006-07
207. Frank Sibley (first spell)	1920-25
208. Ray Harford	1974-77
209. Trevor Francis	1935-39
210. Ned Liddell	1991-94

DAVE THOMAS

211. For which club did Dave sign when he left The R's in 1977?

212. How many League goals did Dave score for QPR in his 41 starts during the 1973/74 season – 4, 5 or 6?

213. In which year was Dave born in Kirkby-in-Ashfield – 1949, 1950 or 1951?

214. How much did QPR pay for Dave when he joined The R's - £165,000, £175,000 or £185,000?

215. How many League goals did Dave score for QPR in his 41 starts during the 1975/76 season – 8, 9 or 10?

216. Which Hoops manager brought Dave to Loftus Road in 1972?

217. Against which team did Dave score his first QPR League goal, in a 3-1 home win during December 1972?

218. How many England caps did Dave win whilst a Hoops player – 8, 18 or 28?

219. From which club did Dave join QPR in 1972?

220. In what position did Dave play during his playing days?

WHERE DID THEY COME FROM? – 2

*Match up the player with the club he left
to join Queens Park Rangers*

221.	Iain Dowie	**Birmingham City**
222.	Bob Hazell	**Liverpool**
223.	Gordon Hill	**Oldham Athletic**
224.	Sammy Lee	**Wolverhampton Wanderers**
225.	Danny Shittu	**Stoke City**
226.	Gavin Peacock (second spell)	**Derby County**
227.	Rowan Vine	**West Ham United**
228.	Robbie James	**Plymouth Argyle**
229.	Jamie Mackie	**Chelsea**
230.	Ted Goodier	**Charlton Athletic**

PHIL PARKES

231. From which Midlands team did Phil sign when he joined QPR in 1970?

232. Against which country did Phil win his one full international cap whilst a QPR player in 1974?

233. For which East Anglian team did Phil make three League appearances during the 1990/91 season?

234. In what position did Phil play during his playing days?

235. In which year was Phil born in Sedgley, West Midlands – 1948, 1949 or 1950?

236. Against which club did Phil make his QPR debut, in a 3-1 home League defeat during August 1970?

237. True or false: Phil once scored a League goal for The R's in his playing career?

238. Phil was a QPR player for nine seasons, but how many times was he an ever-present R's player, appearing in every League match during the season?

239. In 1979, when he left QPR, for which London club did Phil sign for £565,000, a world record transfer fee for a goalkeeper at the time?

240. How many League games did Phil play for QPR in his football career – 322, 344 or 366?

FA CUP WINS

Match up the season/round with Queens Park Rangers' win

241.	1961/62, 1st round replay	QPR 3-1 Leeds United
242.	1977/78, 4th round replay	QPR 2-0 Arsenal
243.	1986/87, 3rd round	QPR 7-0 Barry Town
244.	1965/66, 1st round replay	QPR 3-2 Barnsley
245.	1920/21, 1st round	QPR 5-2 Leicester City
246.	1981/82, 4th round replay	QPR 6-1 West Ham United
247.	1994/95, 5th round	QPR 5-1 Brighton & Hove Albion
248.	1996/97, 4th round	QPR 5-1 Blackpool
249.	1936/37, 1st round	QPR 4-0 Colchester United
250.	1931/32, 3rd round	QPR 1-0 Millwall

DAVID SEAMAN

251. From which club did QPR sign David in 1986?

252. What is David's middle name – Andrew, Adam or Arthur?

253. True or false: David won the first of his 75 full England international caps whilst an R's player?

254. How many League games did David play for QPR in his career - 131, 141 or 151?

255. Where in the UK was David born in 1963 – Rotherham, Leeds or Sheffield?

256. True or false: David once scored a League goal for QPR?

257. Against which team did David make his QPR League debut, in a 5-1 away defeat during August 1986?

258. Which R's manager signed David for the club?

259. True or false: David is left-handed, but threw the football with his right arm and kicked with his right foot?

260. In what year did David leave Loftus Road for Arsenal?

SQUAD NUMBERS 2010/2011 - 2

Match up the player with his squad number

261.	Heidar Helguson	24
262.	Bradley Orr	25
263.	Kaspars Gorkšs	9
264.	Patrick Agyemang	4
265.	Shaun Derry	17
266.	Hogan Ephraim	2
267.	Alejandro Faurlin	6
268.	Lee Cook	13
269.	Mikele Leigertwood	19
270.	Radek Černý	11

PAUL PARKER

271.   In what position did Paul play during his playing days?

272.   From which club did Paul sign for QPR in 1987?

273.   In which year was Paul born in West Ham – 1962, 1963 or 1964?

274.   How many League appearances did Paul make for QPR in his career – 115, 125 or 135?

275.   Paul was appointed manager of which Essex club in 2001?

276.   Which manager signed Paul for Queens Park Rangers?

277.   True or false: Paul won the first of his 19 England international caps whilst a QPR player?

278.   What is Paul's middle name – Adrian, Alan or Andrew?

279.   How many League goals did Paul score for The R's in his playing career – 1, 6 or 11?

280.   In what year did Paul leave Loftus Road and sign for Manchester United?

CAPS FOR MY COUNTRY

Match up the player with the number of caps he won for his country

281.	Dominic Iorfa	9 caps for Scotland
282.	Terry Mancini	27 caps for Venezuela
283.	Kenny Sansom	13 caps for Scotland
284.	Roy Wegerle	21 caps for Nigeria
285.	Iain Dowie	41 caps for USA
286.	Fernando de Ornelas	12 caps for England
287.	Patrick Agyemang	86 caps for England
288.	Frank McLintock	4 caps for Ghana
289.	Alan Brazil	59 caps for Northern Ireland
290.	Andy Sinton	5 caps for Republic of Ireland

ANDY SINTON

291. From which club did Andy sign when he arrived at QPR in 1989?

292. Against which Midlands club did Andy score the only goal in a 1-0 home win during March 1989, in Andy's home League debut?

293. How many League goals did Andy score in his first season at Loftus Road, 1988/89, in his 10 starts?

294. True or false: Andy was the only ever-present QPR player during the 1989/90 League season?

295. Which squad number did Andy wear for QPR during the 1992/93 season?

296. Against which country did Andy make his England international debut, in a 1-1 away draw during November 1991?

297. How much did QPR pay for Andy when he arrived at the club during March 1989?

298. For which club did Andy sign when he left Loftus Road in 1993?

299. For which London team did Andy play between 1996 and 1999?

300. True or false: Andy was the first QPR player in the club's history to score a Premier League hat-trick?

NATIONALITIES – 2

Match up the player with his nationality

301.	Jan Stejskal	Dutch
302.	Marcin Kuś	American
303.	Dexter Blackstock	Finnish
304.	Billy McEwan	Polish
305.	Sampsa Timoska	Czechoslovakian
306.	Alejandro Faurlin	Irish
307.	Mick O'Brien	Congolese
308.	Samuel Koejoe	Scottish
309.	Pat Kanyuka	English
310.	Juergen Sommer	Argentinian

TERRY FENWICK

311. What is Terry's middle name – William, Warren or Wayne?

312. How many full England international caps did Terry win during his playing career – 20, 25 or 30?

313. Which club did Terry join in 1987 when he left The Hoops?

314. Against which Welsh team did Terry score his first QPR League goal, in a 2-0 home win during February 1981?

315. True or false: Terry started and played in all of QPR's 42 League matches during the 1983/84 season?

316. Against which East Anglian team did Terry score a QPR brace, one of them a penalty, in a 3-0 away win during October 1983?

317. Against which team did Terry make his QPR League debut, in a 2-1 away win during December 1980?

318. In which position did Terry play during his playing days – fullback, central midfielder or striker?

319. How much did Terry cost QPR when he joined the club in 1980 - £50,000, £100,000 or £200,000?

320. From which London club did Terry join QPR in 1980?

PLAYING YEARS AT THE CLUB – 1

Match up the player with the years he spent at Queens Park Rangers

321.	Stan Bowles	1997-2007
322.	Danny Dichio	1972-78
323.	Paul Furlong (second spell)	1953-65
324.	Peter Angell	2006-09
325.	Don Givens	1946-53
326.	Gary Micklewhite	1994-97
327.	Billy McEwan	1980-85
328.	Matthew Rose	1938-50
329.	Dexter Blackstock	1972-80
330.	Bill Heath	2002-07

RAY WILKINS

331.   How many of the 70 League games played under Ray's management did QPR win - 25, 27 or 29?

332.   When Ray was appointed player/manager in November 1994 he took the reins from which manager, who went on to manage Tottenham Hotspur?

333.   Against which London team did Ray score his first League goal for QPR, in a 2-0 home win during March 1990?

334.   In what position did Ray play during his playing days?

335.   What is Ray's middle name – Christopher, Colin or Charles?

336.   How many League goals did Ray score for QPR in his 27 League appearances in the club's first Premier League season, 1992/93?

337.   Ray was ever present for QPR in the 1990/91 season along with which other two R's players?

338.   How many League appearances did Ray make for QPR in his football career - 187, 197 or 207?

339.   Against which London team did Ray make his QPR League debut, in a 3-0 away win in December 1989?

340.   How many League goals did Ray score for QPR in his football career – 10, 15 or 20?

POSITIONS THEY PLAYED – 1

*Match up the player with his playing position
at Queens Park Rangers*

341.	John Hollins	Inside forward
342.	Andy Malcolm	Goalkeeper
343.	Lee Harper	Fullback
344.	Roger Morgan	Midfielder
345.	Conway Smith	Centre forward
346.	Arthur Jefferson	Winger
347.	Simon Stainrod	Goalkeeper
348.	Danny Maddix	Forward
349.	Lee Camp	Wing half
350.	Barry Bridges	Central defender

DIVISION TWO CHAMPIONS – 1982/1983

351. How many of their 42 League matches did QPR win – 22, 24 or 26?

352. Who finished as the club's highest League scorer with 16 goals?

353. How many League goals did John Gregory score this season – 10, 15 or 20?

354. Who was in charge of Queens Park Rangers this season?

355. Which team did The R's beat 4-0 at home during October 1982?

356. True or false: QPR won all five League matches during March 1983?

357. Which team did QPR beat 6-1 at home during March 1983, recording their biggest League win of the season?

358. What was the average League attendance this season – 12,806, 13,806 or 14,806?

359. True or false: QPR won the title by 10 clear points at the top of the table?

360. Can you name the three players who were ever presents for QPR during this successful season?

TOP APPEARANCES

Match up the player with the number of competitive appearances he made for QPR

361.	Phil Parkes	457
362.	Ian Gillard	472 (4)
363.	Keith Rutter	476 (7)
364.	Tony Ingham	440
365.	Peter Angell	369
366.	Tony Hazell	467
367.	Dave Clement	406
368.	Archie Mitchell	407 (8)
369.	Mike Keen	479 (5)
370.	Alan McDonald	555

DAVE SEXTON

371. True or false: Dave played for QPR during his playing days?

372. What was Dave awarded in 2005?

373. Which QPR boss did Dave take over from in October 1974?

374. How many of the 115 League matches played while Dave was QPR boss did the club win – 47, 49 or 51?

375. In what year did Dave leave QPR as club manager?

376. Which London club did Dave manage before he took charge at Queens Park Rangers in 1974?

377. To what position in the League did Dave guide QPR during 1974/75, his first season in charge at the club?

378. Which club did Dave manage when he left The R's as club manager?

379. In which year was Dave born in Islington, London – 1930, 1932 or 1934?

380. True or false: Dave only ever managed teams based in England?

PLAYING YEARS AT THE CLUB – 2

*Match up the player with the years he
spent at Queens Park Rangers*

381.	Glenn Roeder	2008-10
382.	Keith Rutter	1986-90
383.	David Seaman	1946-53
384.	Reg Allen	1962-66
385.	Stuart Leary	1993-99
386.	Wayne Routledge	1976-79
387.	Bobby Cameron	1978-84
388.	Steve Yates	1938-50
389.	Peter Eastoe	1950-59
390.	Bert Addinall	1954-63

TERRY VENABLES

411.   Against which club did Terry make his QPR League debut, in a 3-0 home win during August 1969?

412.   How many League goals did Terry score for QPR in his 34 starts during his first season at the club, 1969/70?

413.   In what year was Terry appointed as R's manager?

414.   Which Spanish club did Terry go on to manage when he left Loftus Road as club manager?

415.   From which London club did QPR sign Terry in 1969?

416.   How many of the 153 League games played under Terry's management did the club win – 71, 81 or 91?

417.   True or false: Terry guided the club to the Second Division title during the 1982/83 season?

418.   What number did Terry usually wear whilst a QPR player?

419.   What is Terry's middle name – Frederick, Frank or Francis?

420.   Which manager took over at QPR when Terry left the club as boss in 1984?

TOP GOALSCORERS

Match up the player with the number of goals he scored for QPR

421. Rodney Marsh	*93*
422. Mark Lazarus	*134*
423. Brian Bedford	*96*
424. Stan Bowles	*186*
425. Kevin Gallen	*101*
426. Don Givens	*93*
427. Jimmy Birch	*180*
428. George Goddard	*84*
429. Tommy Cheetham	*144*
430. Cyril Hatton	*97*

IAN HOLLOWAY

431.   What is Ian's nickname?

432.   From which club did QPR sign Ian in 1991?

433.   What squad number did Ian wear for QPR during the
       1993/94 season?

434.   Against which two clubs did Ian score two goals for
       QPR in their first ever Premier League season,
       1992/93?

435.   How many of the 223 League matches played while
       Ian was in charge at QPR did the club win - 93, 94 or
       95?

436.   Which QPR manager did Ian take over from in 2001?

437.   In what position in Division Two did QPR finish during
       the 2001/02 season, Ian's first full season in charge at
       the club?

438.   How much did Ian cost QPR when he joined the club in
       1991 - £225,000, £455,000 or £655,000?

439.   In what position did Ian play during his playing days –
       defender, midfielder or winger?

440.   What is Ian's middle name – Scott, Simon or Stephen?

CLUB RECORDS

441.   Which player scored 44 goals for QPR in the 1966/67 season?

442.   Who is QPR's most capped player, with 52 appearances for Northern Ireland?

443.   How many goals in all competitions did George Goddard score for The R's between 1926 and 1934?

444.   Which player made 519 League appearances for QPR between 1950 and 1963?

445.   Which team did The R's beat 9-2 in Division Three on 3 December 1960 to record their biggest League win?

446.   QPR's highest home attendance was 35,353 on 27 April 1974, in a Division One match against which opponents?

447.   QPR suffered their heaviest League defeat in a Division One match against Manchester United on 19 March 1969, but what was the score?

448.   In 1963 who became the youngest player to play for The R's at the age of 15 years and 275 days?

449.   Which player scored 37 League goals in Division Three South in the 1929/30 season?

450.   Which club paid £6 million for Les Ferdinand in June 1995?

JIM SMITH

451. True or false: Jim played for QPR during his playing days?

452. Which season in the 1980s was Jims first as QPR boss?

453. How many of the 139 matches played under Jim's management did QPR win - 52, 62 or 72?

454. Which club did Jim manage before arriving at Loftus Road?

455. What is Jim's nickname?

456. To what position in Division One did Jim guide QPR in his first season in charge at the club?

457. True or false: Jim's most successful time in the League as QPR manager was when the club finished 5th in Division One during the 1987/88 season?

458. In which year was Jim born in Sheffield – 1938, 1940 or 1942?

459. Which team did Jim go on to manage when he left Loftus Road in 1988?

460. True or false: Jim guided the club to the League Cup final in April 1986?

STAN BOWLES

461. At which Lancashire club, winners of the First Division in 1967/68, did Stan begin his professional career in 1967?

462. Following on from the previous question, Stan left this club to join which team called The Shakers in 1970?

463. In 1970-71 Stan played for which Fourth Division side with an 'x' in their name?

464. What is the title of Stan's autobiography, published in 1996?

465. How many League appearances did Stan make for The Hoops – 235, 245 or 255?

466. Which West London club did Stan join in 1981?

467. Which player did Stan replace at QPR in 1972?

468. Which England manager, in his last game in charge of the national team, gave Stan his first England cap?

469. How many League goals did Stan score in his QPR career – 70, 80 or 90?

470. Stan signed for which reigning European Cup holders in 1979?

QPR V. BRENTFORD

471.   True or false: the clubs did not meet in any competitive competition in the 1970s, 1980s and 1990s?

472.   Which QPR striker scored the only goal in a 1-0 home League win during November 2003?

473.   What was the score when the sides met at Griffin Park during February 2004 in League One?

474.   True or false: QPR once beat Brentford 10-0 in a League match during the 1960s?

475.   Which of the two teams finished higher in Division Three during the 1960/61 season?

476.   What was the score when the two sides met during the 2001/02 season in the League both home and away?

477.   Which R's player scored the only goal in a 1-0 home win in Division Three in January 1966?

478.   Which R's midfielder scored a 90th-minute winner in a 2-1 away win at Brentford in a League One match during April 2003?

479.   In which year did the sides first meet in the FA Cup – 1946, 1947 or 1948?

480.   Which team finished higher in Division Three during the 2002/03 season?

MATCH THE YEAR – 1

Match up the year with the event that took place

481.	Bradley Orr signed for QPR from Bristol City	1988
482.	Alan Mullery became manager of Queens Park Rangers	1894
483.	Queens Park Rangers were Nationwide Division Two runners-up	1965
484.	Queens Park Rangers entered the FA Cup for the first time	1959
485.	Paul Parker joined Manchester United for £1.75 million	2004
486.	Queens Park Rangers became Southern Charity Cup winners	1991
487.	Jim Gregory became Chairman of Queens Park Rangers	1972
488.	Alec Stock became manager of Queens Park Rangers	1984
489.	Rodney Marsh was sold to Manchester City for £200,000	1913
490.	Ian Dawes was transferred to Millwall	2010

NEIL WARNOCK

491. True or false: Neil played for QPR during his playing days?

492. Which team did Neil manage during the 1998/99 season?

493. True or false: Neil is fully qualified as a referee?

494. In what position did Neil play during his playing days?

495. In which year was Neil born in Sheffield – 1946, 1947 or 1948?

496. What was the score when West Bromwich Albion visited Loftus Road just a few days after Neil took over as boss?

497. Which London club did Neil manage before taking over at QPR?

498. In what month during 2010 did Neil take charge at Loftus Road?

499. Neil is a lifelong fan of which team?

500. True or false: Neil was awarded the Manager of the Month award for August 2010 after QPR's great start to the 2010/11 League season?

GERRY FRANCIS

501. Gerry was born on 6 December in which year – 1951, 1953 or 1955?

502. Where was Gerry born – Chiswick, Kew or Putney?

503. At which club did Gerry start his professional career in 1968, remaining there for 11 years?

504. From 1974 to 1976 Gerry played for England at inter national level, but how many appearances did he make for his country – 10, 12 or 14?

505. Gerry captained England on how many occasions – 6, 8 or 10?

506. Who appointed Gerry as England captain in 1975?

507. How many League appearances did Gerry make in his two spells at Queens Park Rangers – 302, 312 or 322?

508. True or false: in 1987 Gerry became player/manager of Bristol Rovers, putting £20,000 of his own money into the club?

509. How many League goals did Gerry score in his QPR career – 37, 47 or 57?

510. In which year did Gerry retire from football management – 2000, 2001 or 2002?

IAN GILLARD

511.   Against which club did Ian score his first QPR League goal, in a 2-1 home win during January 1970?

512.   In which year was Ian born in Hammersmith, London – 1946, 1948 or 1950?

513.   How many competitive goals did Ian score for QPR in his football career – 9, 11 or 13?

514.   What squad number did Ian usually wear for QPR?

515.   In what year did Ian win his three full international caps for England, playing against West Germany, Wales and Czechoslovakia?

516.   Which R's manager handed Ian his club debut?

517.   For which team did Ian sign when he left QPR in July 1982?

518.   In what position did Ian play during his playing days?

519.   Against which club did Ian make his QPR League debut during November 1968?

520.   What is Ian's middle name – Terry, Trevor or Tobias?

HOW MUCH DID THEY PAY? – 1

*Match up the player with the transfer fee
paid by Queens Park Rangers*

521.	Phil Parkes from Walsall, June 1970	£60,000
522.	Stan Bowles from Carlisle United, September 1972	£877,500
523.	John Spencer from Chelsea, November 1996	Free
524.	Les Allen from Tottenham Hotspur, December 1968	£540,000
525.	Jamie Mackie from Plymouth Argyle, May 2010	£112,000
526.	Shaun Derry from Crystal Palace, July 2010	£15,000
527.	Terry Venables from Tottenham Hotspur, June 1969	£990,000
528.	Peter Crouch from Tottenham Hotspur, July 2000	£2,350,000
529.	Paddy Kenny from Sheffield United, July 2010	£70,000
530.	Rob Hulse from Derby County, July 2010	£21,000

QPR V. CHELSEA

531.   Which R's player scored the only goal when QPR beat
       Chelsea 1-0 at home during March 1995?

532.   True or false: QPR beat Chelsea 6-0 at home in Division
       One during March 1986?

533.   In which competition did the sides meet during the
       2009/10 season, with Chelsea winning 1-0 at Stamford
       Bridge?

534.   Who scored QPR's goal in a 1-1 away draw in the
       League during March 1996?

535.   In which competition did QPR beat Chelsea 1-0 at
       home during January 1974?

536.   Which striker scored QPR's only goal in a 1-1 home
       draw against Chelsea in the League during April 1994?

537.   What was the score when Chelsea visited Loftus Road
       for a Division One match during September 1990?

538.   Can you name the two seasons during the 1980s in
       which the sides did not meet in any competition?

539.   How many of the eight Premier League meetings
       between the two sides did QPR win during the 1990s?

540.   What was the score when Chelsea visited Loftus Road
       for a Division One match during December 1989?

MATCH THE YEAR – 2

Match up the year with the event that took place

541.	Stewart Houston became manager of Queens Park Rangers	1950
542.	Queens Park Rangers turned professional	1980
543.	Queens Park Rangers became Division Three South runners-up	2007
544.	Terry Fenwick joined Queens Park Rangers from Crystal Palace	1886
545.	The new Ellerslie Road stand was built	1947
546.	Richard Thompson became the youngest QPR Chairman in the Football League	1961
547.	Ernie Shepherd signed from Hull City	1988
548.	After 304 League appearances for QPR, Pat Woods left to play for Hellenic in Australia	1996
549.	St Judes joined Christchurch Rangers to form Queens Park Rangers	1972
550.	Bernie Ecclestone and Flavio Briatore bought the club	1898

FIRST PREMIER LEAGUE SEASON – 1992/1993

551. In what position in the Premier League did the club finish?

552. How much did a match-day programme cost at Loftus Road during this season?

553. Against which club did QPR play their first ever Premier League match, a 1-1 away draw during August 1992?

554. Which team did QPR beat 5-3 away from home during April 1993, with Les Ferdinand scoring a hat-trick in the game?

555. How many League goals did Les Ferdinand score during this season, finishing as the club's highest scorer?

556. True or false: QPR finished above all other London clubs in the Premier League after playing their 42 League matches?

557. What was the score when Arsenal visited Loftus Road in September 1992 and also when QPR visited Highbury in May 1993?

558. Which defender played in more League matches than any other QPR player during this season, starting 41 matches?

559. Against which club did QPR record a 3-1 home win on the final day of the League season during May 1993?

560. True or false: QPR lost only one of their first eleven League matches of the season?

WHO AM I?

561. I joined QPR in 1959, spending 10 years at the club before joining Luton Town. My son Kevin played for West Ham United and Stoke City.

562. I won the League and FA Cup double with Arsenal in 1971 and joined The R's in 1973, finishing my playing career with them in 1977.

563. I was born in Belfast and played 39 times for Northern Ireland. I played for Arsenal from 1988 to 1997 and then joined QPR.

564. I played at centre half and made 339 League appearances for QPR, only scoring one League goal.

565. I made my one and only appearance for England in 1967 and played for The Hoops from 1975 to 1979. My son Chris is a BBC sports presenter.

566. I won the UEFA Cup with Ipswich Town in 1981 and made only four League appearances for QPR in 1986.

567. I was England's first £1 million player and in 1988 I became player/manager of QPR.

568. I was born in Bethnal Green, London, in October 1960. I began my professional playing career with Tottenham Hotspur and joined The Hoops in 1988.

569. I finished my professional playing career at Loftus Road in 1999 before becoming a Hollywood film star.

570. I spent most of my playing days at Bristol Rovers and in 1991 my former manager Gerry Francis signed me to play for QPR.

QPR V. FULHAM

571. Which of the two teams won their one and only
      meeting in the League Cup, during the 1970/71
      season?

572. Who was QPR's goalkeeper when the teams met at
      Loftus Road in a 0-0 home League draw during
      February 2000?

573. Apart from the League, in which other competition did
      the sides meet during the 1971/72 season?

574. In which Division did the sides meet during the
      1931/32 season?

575. Which R's player scored the club's first goal in a
      Division Two 3-1 win at home during May 1983?

576. True or false: QPR and Fulham did not meet in any
      competitive competition during the 1950s?

577. Which team won both Division Two League matches
      during the 1979/80 season?

578. Which team finished higher in the League during the
      2000/01 season?

579. Which team won both Division Two League matches
      during the 1972/73 season?

580. True or false: QPR and Fulham did not meet in any
      competitive competition during the 1960s?

RODNEY MARSH

581. Rodney was born 11 October 1944 in which Hertfordshire town?

582. At which club did Rodney start his professional playing career in 1962?

583. In March 1966 Rodney joined QPR and in his first full season he played 53 games, scoring how many goals – 24, 34 or 44?

584. Which QPR manager signed Rodney in March 1966?

585. How many appearances in all competitions did Rodney make for QPR – 232, 242 or 252?

586. In 1975 Rodney was signed by Malcolm Allison to play for Manchester City, but what was the transfer fee - £100,000, £150,000 or £200,000?

587. With which two close friends did Rodney play at Fulham in 1976-77?

588. How many goals in all competitions did Rodney score for The Hoops – 114, 124, or 134?

589. How many appearances did Rodney make for England between 1971 and 1973, scoring just the one goal against Wales?

590. Rodney was the manager of which American club in 1980?

1993/1994

591. Which QPR player wore squad number 12 during this season?

592. Which striker scored 7 League goals during this season in his 12 starts and 6 substitute appearances?

593. What was the average home attendance at Loftus Road during this season – 13,228, 14,228 or 15,228?

594. Which striker scored a hat-trick away at Everton in a 3-0 win during November 1993?

595. In what position did QPR finish in the Premier League?

596. Who was the manager of QPR during this season?

597. Which winger scored a brace against Tottenham at White Hart Lane in a 2-1 win on the last day of the League season?

598. Against which team did QPR record their biggest League win of the season, a 5-1 home win during October 1993?

599. How many of their 42 League matches did QPR win – 16, 17 or 18?

600. What squad number did Andrew Impey wear during this season?

DON GIVENS

601. At which club did Don start his professional career in 1969?

602. How many caps did Don earn playing for the Republic of Ireland, scoring 19 goals?

603. From which club did Don join QPR in 1972?

604. Against which country did Don make his international debut in May 1969, in a 2-0 win away from home for the Republic of Ireland?

605. How many League appearances did Don make for The R's – 222, 232 or 242?

606. For which Yorkshire club did Don play in 1981-82, only making 11 League appearances and scoring 3 League goals?

607. Don was born in Limerick, Ireland, on 9 August in which year – 1947, 1949 or 1951?

608. How many goals did Don score in 41 games in the 1972/73 season – 19, 21 or 23?

609. Which Midlands club signed Don in 1978 from QPR?

610. How many League goals did Don score in his Hoops career – 56, 66 or 76?

HAT-TRICKS

611. Which R's player scored a hat-trick against Carlisle United in the League Cup during August 2008?

612. How many hat-tricks were scored by QPR players in the club's first ever Premier League season, 1992/93?

613. True or false: no QPR players scored a hat-trick for the club during the 2005/06, 2006/07 and 2007/08 seasons?

614. Which QPR player scored a hat-trick against Sheffield Wednesday in Division Two during November 1981?

615. Who was the first player in the club's history to score five goals in a game, against Oxford United in the League Cup during October 1967?

616. Against which team did Jamie Cureton score a QPR League hat-trick in the 2004/05 season?

617. Who was the first QPR player to score a hat-trick for the club in top-flight football, in Division One against Derby County during February 1975?

618. Who was the first R's player to score a hat-trick for the club, in October 1899?

619. How many League hat-tricks did Brian Bedford score for QPR during the 1961/62 season?

620. True or false: no QPR players scored a hat-trick for the club during the 1988/89 season?

KEVIN GALLEN

621. Where was Kevin born on 21 September 1975 – Chiswick, Kew or Hammersmith?

622. How many England U21 caps did Kevin win?

623. From which club did QPR re-sign Kevin in 2001?

624. In his two spells with The R's how many goals in all competitions did Kevin score – 77, 87 or 97?

625. In what position did Kevin play in his Hoops career?

626. Which two honours did Kevin win with the MK Dons in 2008?

627. How many League appearances did Kevin make for QPR – 365, 375 or 385?

628. Kevin signed for which Yorkshire club in August 2000?

629. Which Blue Square Conference club did Kevin join in 2009?

630. What did Kevin achieve for the first time in his career on 5 April 2010?

PAUL FURLONG

631. In what position did Paul play during his playing days?

632. Against which club did Paul score a brace for QPR in a 3-0 away League win during March 2003?

633. How many League goals did Paul score for QPR during the 2003/04 season – 12, 14 or 16?

634. True or false: Paul had two loan spells at Loftus Road before he signed permanently during September 2002?

635. Against which team did Paul score the only goal for QPR at Loftus Road in the League One play-off semi-final, 2nd leg, during May 2003?

636. For which London team did Paul play between 1994 and 1996?

637. What is Paul's middle name – Anthony, Arnold or Adam?

638. How many League goals did Paul score in his R's football career – 37, 47 or 57?

639. For which team did Paul sign when he left Loftus Road in August 2007?

640. Against which club did Paul score a brace for QPR, including a 90th-minute winner, in a 3-2 home League win during September 2004?

ALAN McDONALD

641. How many League appearances did Alan make for QPR – 402, 412 or 422?

642. What was Alan's nickname at QPR?

643. In what position did Alan play at The R's?

644. From 1986 to 1996 how many international appearances did Alan make for Northern Ireland, scoring three goals – 32, 42 or 52?

645. How many League goals did Alan score for The Hoops – 13, 16 or 19?

646. At which club did Alan finish his professional playing career in 1998?

647. Alan was the manager of which Irish club from 2007 to 2010?

648. In 2006 Alan became the assistant manager at Loftus Road to which manager?

649. Alan was loaned to which London club in 1983, where he played nine League games?

650. Alan was born in Belfast on 12 October in which year – 1961, 1963 or 1965?

MARC BIRCHAM

651. For which country did Marc win 17 full international caps, scoring one goal?

652. For which club did Marc sign when he left Loftus Road in 2007?

653. Against which club did Marc score his first QPR League goal, in a 1-1 home draw during December 2002?

654. How many League goals did Marc score for QPR during the 2003/04 season?

655. Which R's manager purchased Marc for the club?

656. True or false: Marc was appointed QPR youth coach at the start of the 2008/09 season?

657. In which year was Marc born in Brent – 1976, 1978 or 1980?

658. In what position did Marc play during his playing days?

659. How many League goals did Marc score in his QPR career – 7, 17 or 27?

660. From which London team did Marc sign when he joined QPR in 2002?

DAVE CLEMENT

661. Against which country did Dave make his England debut, coming on as a substitute at half-time, in a 2-1 England win during March 1976?

662. How many League appearances did Dave make for The Hoops – 387, 397 or 407?

663. In what position did Dave play at QPR?

664. Which club paid £170,000 for Dave in 1979?

665. How many League goals did Dave score for The R's – 21, 31 or 41?

666. Dave was born in Battersea on 2 February in which year – 1946, 1948 or 1950?

667. At which club did Dave finish his professional playing career, after suffering a broken leg in 1982?

668. From the 1970/71 season to the 1973/74 season how many QPR League games did Dave miss – 6, 8 or 10?

669. True or false: Dave's son Neil spent most of his professional career playing for Chelsea?

670. How many England international caps did Dave win – 1, 3 or 5?

STADIUMS

671.   True or false: in October 1953 floodlights were used at Loftus Road for the first time for a friendly game against Arsenal?

672.   Which London team shared Loftus Road with QPR between 2002 and 2004 while their ground was being redeveloped?

673.   Which two countries shared a 1-1 draw in an international match played at Loftus Road during November 2005?

674.   At which stadium did QPR play their home games during the 1962/63 season?

675.   True or false: in June 1985 Barry McGuigan successfully challenged Eusebio Pedroza to become WBA world featherweight boxing champion at Loftus Road?

676.   Which rugby union team used Loftus Road as their home ground from 1996/97 until 2001/02?

677.   What is the club's postcode?

678.   What is the size of the Loftus Road pitch - 112 x 72 yards, 114 x 74 yards or 116 x 76 yards?

679.   In which year was Loftus Road built – 1900, 1902 or 1904?

680.   Can you name the four stands currently at Loftus Road?

MICK LEACH

681. How many appearances in all competitions did Mick make for The R's – 317, 327 or 337?

682. In March 1978 Mick joined Detroit Express, for what transfer fee - £30,000, £40,000 or £50,000?

683. Mick made his debut for QPR in February 1965, scoring a goal in a 5-0 home win against which Essex club?

684. In what two positions did Mick play at QPR?

685. In February 1976 Mick was given a testimonial match at Loftus Road against which European club?

686. How many League goals did Mick score in his R's career – 41, 51 or 61?

687. Mick was born in Clapton on 16 January in which year – 1943, 1945 or 1947?

688. At which club did Mick finish his professional playing career in 1979?

689. True or false: Mick served as an apprentice at QPR before signing as a professional?

690. For how many years did Mick play for The R's?

LEAGUE CUP WINNERS – 1967

691.   Which team did QPR beat in the final?

692.   What was the score in the final?

693.   What was the attendance in the final, played at Wembley Stadium – 77,952, 87,952 or 97,952?

694.   Which Midlands team did QPR beat 7-2 on aggregate in the League Cup semi-finals?

695.   Who captained The R's to victory in the final?

696.   Can you name the QPR player who scored the club's winning goal in the final, in the 81st minute?

697.   In which Division were QPR when they won this competition?

698.   True or false: this was the first final to be decided over a single game, the six previous finals having been contested over two legs?

699.   Which manager led the club to this success?

700.   What was the score at half-time?

HOW MUCH DID THEY PAY? – 2

*Match up the player with the transfer
fee paid by Queens Park Rangers*

701.	Jan Stejskal from Sparta Prague, October 1990	£4,000
702.	Tony Currie from Leeds United, May 1979	£15,000
703.	Rodney Marsh from Fulham, March 1966	£650,000
704.	Kevin Gallen from Barnsley, November 2001	£750,000
705.	Trevor Sinclair from Blackpool, August 1993	£10,000
706.	Ian Watson from Chelsea, July 1965	£390,000
707.	Mike Sheron from Stoke City, July 1997	£35,000
708.	Don Shanks from Luton Town, November 1974	£2,350,000
709.	Keith Sanderson from Plymouth Argyle, June 1965	£625,000
710.	Steve Yates from Bristol Rovers, August 1993	Free

DIVISION ONE RUNNERS-UP – 1975/1976

711.   How much was a match-day programme at Loftus Road during the 1975/76 season?

712.   Which team beat QPR to the title by only one point in Division One?

713.   Against which team did QPR record their biggest win of the League season, a 5-0 home win during October 1975, with Gerry Francis scoring a hat-trick?

714.   Can you name the only two players that played in all 42 League matches during this season?

715.   With how many League goals did Don Givens end the season, finishing as the club's highest scorer?

716.   True or false: QPR lost only one of their last 15 League matches of the season?

717.   How many of their 42 League matches did the club win during this season - 24, 25 or 26?

718.   True or false: QPR were unbeaten in their five League matches during November 1975?

719.   Which team did QPR beat 2-0 at home on the opening day of the League season?

720.   Which R's player scored a brace in a 3-0 away win at Tottenham during February 1976?

MIKE KEEN

721.   Mike made his Hoops debut in a 2-1 away defeat in September 1959, against which club?

722.   How many League appearances did Mike make for QPR – 390, 393 or 396?

723.   In what position did Mike play?

724.   At what club did Mike finish his professional playing career in 1975, going on to manage them?

725.   True or false: Mike ran a sports shop in High Wycombe in the 1970s and '80s?

726.   When Mike left QPR in 1969, which club did he join for £18,500?

727.   How many League goals did Mike score for The R's – 19, 29 or 39?

728.   What was Mike's middle name – Terry, Thomas or Timothy?

729.   Mike was the manager of which club from 1980 to 1984?

730.   True or false: Mike was captain of the QPR side that won the League Cup and Third Division Championship in 1967?

LEGENDS - 1

Rearrange the letters to reveal the name of a club legend

731. OTYN NAGHIM

732. REGEGO ODDGRAD

733. ENVIK NAGELL

734. HONJ RYEGROG

735. ANI WHOLOYAL

736. YNDA ISNTNO

737. LIPH ASKREP

738. RETYR NICKFEW

739. RAGHER THROWINSA

740. TRYER NABELVES

LEAGUE APPEARANCES

Match up the player with the number of League appearances he made for QPR

741. David Bardsley	67
742. Karl Ready	96
743. Conway Smith	29
744. Gareth Ainsworth	226
745. Marcus Bignot	141
746. Clarke Carlisle	253
747. Trevor Francis	182
748. Terrell Forbes	32
749. Frank Clarke	174
750. Peter Reid	114

PLAYING AWAY

*Which team would be QPR's opponents if they
visited the following grounds*

751. Britannia Stadium

752. Ricoh Arena

753. Ashton Gate

754. The Liberty Stadium

755. Keepmoat Stadium

756. Boundary Park

757. Prenton Park

758. Glanford Park

759. The Walkers Stadium

760. Bramall Lane

BRIAN BEDFORD

761. True or false: Brian's first name was Noel but he preferred to use his middle name of Brian?

762. At which club did Brian start his professional playing career in April 1954?

763. How many League appearances did Brian make for The R's – 238, 248 or 258?

764. Brian made his debut for QPR in August 1959 in a 2-0 win against which club?

765. Following on from the previous question, which club did Brian sign from for £750 to join QPR?

766. At which London club did Brian finish his League playing career in England before going to the USA to join the Atlanta Chiefs in 1967?

767. How many League goals did Brian score for The R's – 151, 161 or 171?

768. In what position did Brian play?

769. What nationality was Brian – English, Scottish or Welsh?

770. Which team did Brian join when he left QPR in 1965, scoring 23 League goals in 37 League appearances for his new club?

LEGENDS – 2

Rearrange the letters to reveal the name of a club legend

771. YONDER HARMS

772. ADEV SHOTMA

773. GREYR INSCARF

774. ADDIV AMSANE

775. YAR WINSILK

776. LANA DAMNCOLD

777. LUPA ARKREP

778. SLE ANDFRIEND

779. TANS ELBOWS

780. VETORR NAILRISC

LEAGUE GOALSCORERS

Match up the player with the number of League goals he scored for QPR

781. Gary Bannister	28
782. Terry Mancini	16
783. Simon Stainrod	3
784. Terry Venables	30
785. George Petchey	48
786. Trevor Sinclair	51
787. John Byrne	22
788. Tony Sealy	56
789. Dave Thomas	18
790. Ernie Shepherd	19

FA CUP RUNNERS-UP - 1982

791.   Which team did QPR beat 1-0 in the FA Cup semi-final, played at Highbury?

792.   What was the score when Tottenham beat QPR in the FA Cup final replay?

793.   Which R's player scored the club's goal against Tottenham in the FA Cup final, resulting in a 1-1 draw?

794.   Can you name the goalkeeper that played for QPR in both the final and final replay?

795.   Which manager led QPR to this FA Cup final?

796.   True or false: QPR and Tottenham played the FA Cup final replay exactly a week after the final?

797.   Which London club did QPR beat 1-0 at home in the quarter-finals?

798.   Who was the only non-Englishman in QPR's starting eleven in the FA Cup final and replay?

799.   Which R's player captained the team in the final replay as Glenn Roeder was suspended for this match?

800.   By what scoreline did QPR beat Blackpool at home in the 5th round replay?

ANSWERS

CLUB HISTORY

1.   *1882*
2.   *Loftus Road*
3.   *Dave Mangnall*
4.   *The Hoops, Rangers and The R's*
5.   *Tottenham Hotspur*
6.   *West Bromwich Albion*
7.   *19,100*
8.   *Clive Allen*
9.   *Partizan Belgrade*
10.   *Neil Warnock*

2010/2011

11.   *Clint Hill*
12.   *Tommy Smith*
13.   *Barnsley*
14.   *Ipswich Town*
15.   *Jamie Mackie*
16.   *Kaspars Gorkšs*
17.   *True: 3 wins and 1 draw*
18.   *0-0*
19.   *Rob Hulse*
20.   *Adel Taarabt*

CLUB HONOURS

21.	*Division Two Champions*	*1983*
22.	*Division Three Champions*	*1967*
23.	*Southern League Champions*	*1912*
24.	*Division Three South Champions*	*1948*
25.	*FA Cup Runners-Up*	*1982*
26.	*London Cup Winners*	*1895*
27.	*League Cup Winners*	*1967*

28.	Western League Champions	1906
29.	League Cup Runners-Up	1986
30.	Division One Runners-Up	1976

TONY INGHAM

31.	True
32.	514
33.	Commercial director
34.	Leeds United
35.	True
36.	3
37.	Doncaster Rovers
38.	Defender
39.	1925
40.	False: he never played for England

WHERE DID THEY COME FROM? – 1

41.	Leighton James	Burnley
42.	Ian Holloway	Bristol Rovers
43.	Gary Penrice	Watford
44.	David Webb	Leicester City
45.	Kenny Sansom	Coventry City
46.	Trevor Francis	Sheffield Wednesday
47.	David Bardsley	Blackpool
48.	John Hollins	Arsenal
49.	Nigel Quashie (first spell)	Nottingham Forest
50.	Roy Wegerle	Blackburn Rovers

GEORGE GODDARD

51.	Centre forward
52.	177
53.	True: with 186 goals

54.	1926
55.	Redhill
56.	1903
57.	True: he signed for them in July 1935
58.	The club needed the money
59.	Brentford
60.	37

MANAGERS – 1

61.	Ian Holloway	2001-06
62.	James Cowan	1907-13
63.	Gordon Jago	1971-74
64.	Terry Venables	1980-84
65.	Alec Stock	1959-68
66.	Ray Wilkins	1994-96
67.	Jack Taylor	1952-59
68.	Don Howe	1989-91
69.	Gerry Francis (second spell)	1998-2001
70.	Jim Smith	1985-88

2009/2010

71.	Bristol City
72.	Crystal Palace
73.	14
74.	Blackpool
75.	Mikele Leigertwood
76.	4-2 to QPR
77.	Radek Černý (29 games) and Carl Ikeme (17 games)
78.	Jay Simpson
79.	Wayne Routledge
80.	13th

NATIONALITIES – 1

81.	Danny Shittu	Nigerian
82.	Roy Wegerle	American
83.	Gino Padula	Argentinian
84.	Kaspars Gorkšs	Latvian
85.	Luděk Mikloško	Czechoslovakian
86.	Adel Taarabt	Moroccan
87.	Georges Santos	French
88.	Ned Zelić	Australian
89.	Chris Kiwomya	English
90.	Sieb Dijkstra	Dutch

2008/2009

91.	15
92.	Iain Dowie
93.	Heidar Helguson
94.	Blackpool
95.	11th
96.	11
97.	False: won 2, drew 2 and lost 1
98.	Sheffield Wednesday
99.	Dexter Blackstock
100.	Charlton Athletic

WHERE DID THEY COME FROM? – 1

101.	Tony Currie	Leeds United
102.	Ákos Buzsáky	Plymouth Argyle
103.	Roy Faulkner	Blackburn Rovers
104.	Frank McLintock	Arsenal
105.	Don Masson	Notts County
106.	Fitz Hall	Wigan Athletic
107.	Martin Rowlands	Brentford

108.	Vinnie Jones	Wimbledon
109.	Mark Hateley	Rangers
110.	Clive Allen (second spell)	Crystal Palace

2007/2008

111.	Leicester City
112.	Mikele Leigertwood
113.	Bristol City
114.	Lee Camp
115.	7
116.	Fitz Hall
117.	Patrick Agyemang
118.	Norwich City
119.	14
120.	Steve Lomas

POSITIONS IN THE LEAGUE – 1

121.	1971/72, 54 points	4th
122.	1991/92, 54 points	11th
123.	1949/50, 34 points	20th
124.	1957/58, 50 points	10th
125.	1979/80, 49 points	5th
126.	1982/83, 85 points	1st
127.	1913/14, 41 points	8th
128.	1928/29, 52 points	6th
129.	2005/06, 50 points	21st
130.	2000/01, 40 points	23rd

2006/2007

131.	18th
132.	12,936
133.	Paul Furlong

134. **Martin Rowlands**

135. **Adam Bolder**

136. **Danny Shittu**

137. **Dexter Blackstock**

138. **John Gregory**

139. **True: won 1, drew 3 and lost 4**

140. **14**

POSITIONS IN THE LEAGUE – 2

141.	2002/03, 83 points	4th
142.	1988/89, 53 points	9th
143.	1966/67, 67 points	1st
144.	1995/96, 33 points	19th
145.	1975/76, 59 points	2nd
146.	1932/33, 37 points	16th
147.	1901/02, 23 points	12th
148.	2004/05, 62 points	11th
149.	1968/69, 18 points	22nd
150.	1954/55, 44 points	15th

LEAGUE CUP RUNNERS-UP 1985/1986

151. **Liverpool**

152. **Chelsea**

153. **Oxford United**

154. **Jim Smith**

155. **Paul Barron**

156. **John Byrne and Michael Robinson**

157. **April (20th)**

158. **Nottingham Forest**

159. **The Milk Cup**

160. **Hull City**

SQUAD NUMBERS 2010/2011 - 1

161.	Fitz Hall	5
162.	Jamie Mackie	12
163.	Paddy Kenny	1
164.	Rob Hulse	20
165.	Adel Taarabt	7
166.	Martin Rowlands	14
167.	Clint Hill	3
168.	Peter Ramage	22
169.	Ákos Buzsáky	10
170.	Leon Clarke	8

LES FERDINAND

171.	Coventry City
172.	24
173.	Newcastle United
174.	True
175.	Hayes
176.	5
177.	Sir Les
178.	Striker
179.	1966
180.	80

WHERE DID THEY GO? – 2

181.	Steve Hodge	Watford
182.	Clive Walker	Fulham
183.	Dean Sturridge	Kidderminster Harriers
184.	Dennis Oli	Swansea City
185.	Andy Impey	West Ham United
186.	Nigel Spackman	Rangers
187.	Glenn Roeder	Newcastle United

188.	Andy Tillson	Bristol Rovers
189.	Eddie Kelly	Leicester City
190.	Ernie Howe	Portsmouth

TREVOR SINCLAIR

191.	Blackpool
192.	Lloyd
193.	True
194.	12 (for England)
195.	Sheffield United
196.	4
197.	Stockport County
198.	£750,000
199.	11
200.	West Ham United

MANAGERS – 2

201.	Dave Sexton	1974-77
202.	Gerry Francis (first spell)	1991-94
203.	Robert Hewison	1925-31
204.	John Gregory	2006-07
205.	Billy Birrell	1935-39
206.	James Howie	1913-20
207.	Frank Sibley (first spell)	1977-78
208.	Ray Harford	1997-98
209.	Trevor Francis	1988-89
210.	Ned Liddell	1920-25

DAVE THOMAS

211.	Everton
212.	6
213.	1950

214.   £165,000

215.   9

216.   Gordon Jago

217.   Leyton Orient

218.   8

219.   Burnley

220.   Left winger

WHERE DID THEY COME FROM? – 2

221.	Iain Dowie	West Ham United
222.	Bob Hazell	Wolverhampton Wanderers
223.	Gordon Hill	Derby County
224.	Sammy Lee	Liverpool
225.	Danny Shittu	Charlton Athletic
226.	Gavin Peacock (second spell)	Chelsea
227.	Rowan Vine	Birmingham City
228.	Robbie James	Stoke City
229.	Jamie Mackie	Plymouth Argyle
230.	Ted Goodier	Oldham Athletic

PHIL PARKES

231.   Walsall

232.   Portugal

233.   Ipswich Town

234.   Goalkeeper

235.   1950

236.   Leicester City

237.   False: he never scored a League goal for any team in his career

238.   3: 1971/72, 1973/74 and 1975/76

239.   West Ham United

240.   344

FA CUP WINS

241.	1961/62, 1st round replay	QPR 7-0 Barry Town
242.	1997/78, 4th round replay	QPR 6-1 West Ham United
243.	1986/87, 3rd round	QPR 5-2 Leicester City
244.	1965/66, 1st round replay	QPR 4-0 Colchester United
245.	1920/21, 1st round	QPR 2-0 Arsenal
246.	1981/82, 4th round replay	QPR 5-1 Blackpool
247.	1994/95, 5th round	QPR 1-0 Millwall
248.	1996/97, 4th round	QPR 3-2 Barnsley
249.	1936/37, 1st round	QPR 5-1 Brighton & Hove Albion
250.	1931/32, 3rd round	QPR 3-1 Leeds United

DAVID SEAMAN

251. Birmingham City
252. Andrew
253. True: against Saudi Arabia in November 1988
254. 141
255. Rotherham
256. False: he never scored a League goal for any club in his career
257. Southampton
258. Jim Smith
259. True
260. 1990

SQUAD NUMBERS 2010/2011 - 2

261.	Heidar Helguson	9
262.	Bradley Orr	2
263.	Kaspars Gorkšs	13
264.	Patrick Agyemang	19
265.	Shaun Derry	4
266.	Hogan Ephraim	25

267.	Alejandro Faurlin	11
268.	Lee Cook	17
269.	Mikele Leigertwood	6
270.	Radek Černý	24

PAUL PARKER

271.	Right back
272.	Fulham
273.	1964
274.	125
275.	Chelmsford City
276.	Jim Smith
277.	True: against Albania in 1989
278.	Andrew
279.	1
280.	1991

CAPS FOR MY COUNTRY

281.	Dominic Iorfa	21 caps for Nigeria
282.	Terry Mancini	5 caps for Republic of Ireland
283.	Kenny Sansom	86 caps for England
284.	Roy Wegerle	41 caps for USA
285.	Iain Dowie	59 caps for Northern Ireland
286.	Fernando de Ornelas	27 caps for Venezuela
287.	Patrick Agyemang	4 caps for Ghana
288.	Frank McLintock	9 caps for Scotland
289.	Alan Brazil	13 caps for Scotland
290.	Andy Sinton	12 caps for England

ANDY SINTON

291.	Brentford

292.	Aston Villa

293.	3

294.	True

295.	11

296.	Poland

297.	£300,000

298.	Sheffield Wednesday

299.	Tottenham Hotspur

300.	True: during December 1992, in a 4-2 home win against Everton

NATIONALITIES – 2

301.	Jan Stejskal	Czechoslovakian
302.	Marcin Kuś	Polish
303.	Dexter Blackstock	English
304.	Billy McEwan	Scottish
305.	Sampsa Timoska	Finnish
306.	Alejandro Faurlin	Argentinian
307.	Mick O'Brien	Irish
308.	Samuel Koejoe	Dutch
309.	Pat Kanyuka	Congolese
310.	Juergen Sommer	American

TERRY FENWICK

311.	William

312.	20

313.	Tottenham Hotspur

314.	Cardiff City

315.	False: he missed the first match of the season against Manchester United, but played in the other 41 matches

316.	Norwich City

317.	Bolton Wanderers

318.	Fullback

319.	£100,000

320.	Crystal Palace

PLAYING YEARS AT THE CLUB – 1

321.	Stan Bowles	1972-80
322.	Danny Dichio	1994-97
323.	Paul Furlong (second spell)	2002-07
324.	Peter Angell	1953-65
325.	Don Givens	1972-78
326.	Gary Micklewhite	1980-85
327.	Billy McEwan	1938-50
328.	Matthew Rose	1997-2007
329.	Dexter Blackstock	2006-09
330.	Bill Heath	1946-53

RAY WILKINS

331.	25

332.	Gerry Francis

333.	Arsenal

334.	Central midfielder

335.	Colin

336.	2

337.	David Bardsley and Andy Sinton

338.	207: 200 (7)

339.	Crystal Palace

340.	10

POSITIONS THEY PLAYED – 1

341.	John Hollins	Midfielder
342.	Andy Malcolm	Wing half
343.	Lee Harper	Goalkeeper
344.	Roger Morgan	Winger

345.	Conway Smith	Inside forward
346.	Arthur Jefferson	Fullback
347.	Simon Stainrod	Forward
348.	Danny Maddix	Central defender
349.	Lee Camp	Goalkeeper
350.	Barry Bridges	Centre forward

DIVISION TWO CHAMPIONS – 1982/1983

351. 26

352. Tony Sealy

353. 15

354. Terry Venables

355. Shrewsbury Town

356. False: 4 wins and 1 defeat

357. Middlesbrough

358. 12,806

359. True: QPR finished top with 85 points; Wolves finished second
with 75 points

360. Peter Hucker, John Gregory and Ian Dawes

TOP APPEARANCES

361.	Phil Parkes	406
362.	Ian Gillard	479 (5)
363.	Keith Rutter	369
364.	Tony Ingham	555
365.	Peter Angell	457
366.	Tony Hazell	407 (8)
367.	Dave Clement	472 (4)
368.	Archie Mitchell	467
369.	Mike Keen	440
370.	Alan McDonald	476 (7)

DAVE SEXTON

371.   *False: he never played for QPR*

372.   *The OBE*

373.   *George Jago*

374.   *51*

375.   *1977*

376.   *Chelsea*

377.   *11th*

378.   *Manchester United*

379.   *1930*

380.   *True*

PLAYING YEARS AT THE CLUB – 2

381.	**Glenn Roeder**	*1978-84*
382.	**Keith Rutter**	*1954-63*
383.	**David Seaman**	*1986-90*
384.	**Reg Allen**	*1938-50*
385.	**Stuart Leary**	*1962-66*
386.	**Wayne Routledge**	*2008-10*
387.	**Bobby Cameron**	*1950-59*
388.	**Steve Yates**	*1993-99*
389.	**Peter Eastoe**	*1976-79*
390.	**Bert Addinall**	*1946-53*

DIVISION TWO RUNNERS-UP 2003/2004

391.   *Plymouth Argyle*

392.   *Ian Holloway*

393.   *Blackpool*

394.   *Kevin Gallen*

395.   *Martin Rowlands*

396.   *Paul Furlong*

397.   *True: 4 wins and 1 draw*

398.   Jamie Cureton

399.   22

400.   14,811

POSITIONS THEY PLAYED – 2

401.	Dave Thomas	Winger
402.	Ian Watson	Fullback
403.	Darren Peacock	Central defender
404.	Harry Brown	Goalkeeper
405.	John Gregory	Midfielder
406.	Des Farrow	Wing half
407.	Gary Waddock	Midfielder
408.	Don Mills	Inside forward
409.	Chris Woods	Goalkeeper
410.	Rufus Brevett	Fullback

TERRY VENABLES

411.   Hull City

412.   5

413.   1980

414.   Barcelona

415.   Tottenham Hotspur

416.   81

417.   True

418.   4

419.   Frederick

420.   Alan Mullery

TOP GOALSCORERS

421.	Rodney Marsh	134
422.	Mark Lazarus	84
423.	Brian Bedford	180

424.	Stan Bowles	96
425.	Kevin Gallen	97
426.	Don Givens	101
427.	Jimmy Birch	144
428.	George Goddard	186
429.	Tommy Cheetham	93
430.	Cyril Hatton	93

IAN HOLLOWAY

431. Ollie

432. Bristol Rovers

433. 8

434. Tottenham Hotspur (home) and Sheffield United (away)

435. 93

436. Gerry Francis

437. 8th

438. £225,000

439. Midfielder

440. Scott

CLUB RECORDS

441. Rodney Marsh (League 30, FA Cup 3 and League Cup 11)

442. Alan McDonald

443. 186

444. Tony Ingham

445. Tranmere Rovers

446. Leeds United

447. QPR 1-8 Manchester United

448. Frank Sibley

449. George Goddard

450. Newcastle United

JIM SMITH

451.   False: he never played for QPR

452.   1985/86

453.   52

454.   Oxford United

455.   The Bald Eagle

456.   13th (1985/86)

457.   True

458.   1940

459.   Newcastle United

460.   True: losing 3-0 to Oxford United

STAN BOWLES

461.   Manchester City

462.   Bury

463.   Crewe Alexandra

464.   Stan the Man

465.   255

466.   Brentford

467.   Rodney Marsh

468.   Sir Alf Ramsey (v. Portugal, April 1974)

469.   70

470.   Nottingham Forest

QPR V. BRENTFORD

471.   True

472.   Tony Thorpe

473.   1-1

474.   False

475.   QPR (QPR 3rd; Brentford 17th)

476.   0-0

477.   Roger Morgan

478. Marc Bircham

479. 1946 (February)

480. QPR (QPR 4th; Brentford 16th)

MATCH THE YEAR – 1

481. Bradley Orr signed for QPR from Bristol City   2010

482. Alan Mullery became manager of
     Queens Park Rangers   1984

483. Queens Park Rangers were Nationwide Division
     Two runners-up   2004

484. Queens Park Rangers entered the FA Cup
     for the first time   1894

485. Paul Parker joined Manchester United
     for £1.75 million   1991

486. Queens Park Rangers became Southern
     Charity Cup winners   1913

487. Jim Gregory became Chairman of
     Queens Park Rangers   1965

488. Alec Stock became manager of
     Queens Park Rangers   1959

489. Rodney Marsh was sold to Manchester City for
     £200,000   1972

490. Ian Dawes was transferred to Millwall   1988

NEIL WARNOCK

491. False: Neil never played for QPR

492. Bury

493. True

494. Winger

495. 1948

496. 3-1 to QPR

497. Crystal Palace

498.   March

499.   Sheffield United

500.   True

GERRY FRANCIS

501.   1951

502.   Chiswick

503.   Queens Park Rangers

504.   12

505.   8

506.   Don Revie

507.   312

508.   True

509.   57

510.   2001

IAN GILLARD

511.   Cardiff City

512.   1950

513.   11

514.   3

515.   1975

516.   Jim Smith

517.   Aldershot

518.   Left back

519.   Nottingham Forest

520.   Terry

HOW MUCH DID THEY PAY? – 1

521.	Phil Parkes from Walsall, June 1970	£15,000
522.	Stan Bowles from Carlisle United, September 1972	£112,000
523.	John Spencer from Chelsea, November 1996	£2,350,000

524.	Les Allen from Tottenham Hotspur, December 1968	£21,000
525.	Jamie Mackie from Plymouth Argyle, May 2010	£540,000
526.	Shaun Derry from Crystal Palace, July 2010	Free
527.	Terry Venables from Tottenham Hotspur, June 1969	£70,000
528.	Peter Crouch from Tottenham Hotspur, July 2000	£60,000
529.	Paddy Kenny from Sheffield United, July 2010	£990,000
530.	Rob Hulse from Derby County, July 2010	£877,500

QPR V. CHELSEA

531. Kevin Gallen

532. True

533. League Cup

534. Simon Barker

535. FA Cup (3rd round replay)

536. Les Ferdinand

537. 1-0 to QPR

538. 1983/84 and 1988/89

539. 1

540. 4-2 to QPR

MATCH THE YEAR – 2

541.	Stewart Houston became manager of Queens Park Rangers	1996
542.	Queens Park Rangers turned professional	1898
543.	Queens Park Rangers became Division Three South runners-up	1947
544.	Terry Fenwick joined Queens Park Rangers from Crystal Palace	1980
545.	The new Ellerslie Road stand was built	1972
546.	Richard Thompson became the youngest QPR Chairman in the Football League	1988
547.	Ernie Shepherd signed from Hull City	1950

548. *After 304 League appearances for QPR, Pat Woods left to play for Hellenic in Australia*   **1961**

549. *St Judes joined Christchurch Rangers to form Queens Park Rangers*   **1886**

550. *Bernie Ecclestone and Flavio Briatore bought the club*   **2007**

FIRST PREMIER LEAGUE SEASON – 1992/1993

551.   **5th**

552.   **£1.30**

553.   **Manchester City**

554.   **Everton**

555.   **20**

556.   **True: only Manchester United, Aston Villa, Norwich City and Blackburn Rovers finished above The R's**

557.   **0-0**

558.   **Clive Wilson**

559.   **Sheffield Wednesday**

560.   **True: losing 1-0 away to Chelsea during August 1992**

WHO AM I?

561.   **Mike Keen**

562.   **Frank McLintock**

563.   **Steve Morrow**

564.   **Keith Rutter**

565.   **John Hollins**

566.   **Alan Brazil**

567.   **Trevor Francis**

568.   **Mark Falco**

569.   **Vinnie Jones**

570.   **Gary Penrice**

QPR V. FULHAM

571. *Fulham (2-0)*

572. *Lee Harper*

573. *FA Cup*

574. *Third Division South*

575. *John Gregory*

576. *True*

577. *QPR (3-0 at home and 2-0 away)*

578. *Fulham (Fulham 1st and QPR 23rd in Division One)*

579. *QPR (2-0 at home and 2-0 away)*

580. *True*

RODNEY MARSH

581. *Hatfield*

582. *Fulham*

583. *44*

584. *Alec Stock*

585. *242*

586. *£200,000*

587. *George Best and Bobby Moore*

588. *134*

589. *9*

590. *New York United*

1993/1994

591. *Gary Penrice*

592. *Devon White*

593. *14,228*

594. *Bradley Allen*

595. *9th*

596. *Gerry Francis*

597. *Trevor Sinclair*

598. Coventry City

599. 16

600. 7

DON GIVENS

601. Manchester United

602. 56

603. Luton Town

604. Denmark

605. 242

606. Sheffield United

607. 1949

608. 23

609. Birmingham City

610. 76

HAT-TRICKS

611. Emmanuel Ledesma

612. 3: Andy Sinton (1) and Les Ferdinand (2)

613. True

614. Simon Stainrod

615. Alan Wilks

616. Coventry City

617. Don Givens

618. Peter Turnbull (against West Hampstead in the FA Cup)

619. 5

620. True

KEVIN GALLEN

621. Chiswick

622. 3

623. Barnsley

624. 97

625. Striker

626. League Two Winners and Football League Trophy Winners

627. 365

628. Huddersfield Town

629. Luton Town

630. He scored his first ever hat-trick in a 6-0 win over Grays Athletic

PAUL FURLONG

631. Striker

632. Huddersfield Town

633. 16

634. True: August-October 2000 and August-September 2002

635. Oldham Athletic

636. Chelsea

637. Anthony

638. 57

639. Luton Town

640. Leicester City

ALAN McDONALD

641. 402

642. Macca

643. Central defender

644. 52

645. 13

646. Swindon Town

647. Glentoran

648. Gary Waddock

649. Charlton Athletic

650. 1963

MARC BIRCHAM

651.   Canada

652.   Yeovil Town

653.   Brentford

654.   2

655.   Ian Holloway

656.   False: it was the start of the 2009/10 season

657.   1978

658.   Midfielder

659.   7

660.   Millwall

DAVE CLEMENT

661.   Wales

662.   407

663.   Right fullback

664.   Bolton Wanderers

665.   21

666.   1948

667.   Fulham

668.   6

669.   False: West Bromwich Albion

670.   5

STADIUMS

671.   True

672.   Fulham

673.   Australia and Ghana

674.   White City Stadium

675.   True

676.   London Wasps

677.   W12 7PJ

678. *112 x 72 yards*

679. *1904*

680. *South Africa Road Stand, School End, Ellerslie Road Stand and Loftus Road End*

MICK LEACH

681. *337*

682. *£30,000*

683. *Colchester United*

684. *Initially a forward, and then a midfielder*

685. *Red Star Belgrade*

686. *61*

687. *1947*

688. *Cambridge United*

689. *True*

690. *13 (1965-78)*

LEAGUE CUP WINNERS – 1967

691. *West Bromwich Albion*

692. *3-2 to QPR*

693. *97,952*

694. *Birmingham City*

695. *Mike Keen*

696. *Mark Lazarus*

697. *Third Division (and West Bromwich Albion were in the First Division)*

698. *True*

699. *Alec Stock*

700. *2-0 to West Bromwich Albion*

HOW MUCH DID THEY PAY? – 2

701. *Jan Stejskal from Sparta Prague, October 1990*   *£625,000*

702.	Tony Currie from Leeds United, May 1979	£390,000
703.	Rodney Marsh from Fulham, March 1966	£15,000
704.	Kevin Gallen from Barnsley, November 2001	Free
705.	Trevor Sinclair from Blackpool, August 1993	£750,000
706.	Ian Watson from Chelsea, July 1965	£10,000
707.	Mike Sheron from Stoke City, July 1997	£2,350,000
708.	Don Shanks from Luton Town, November 1974	£35,000
709.	Keith Sanderson from Plymouth Argyle, June 1965	£4,000
710.	Steve Yates from Bristol Rovers, August 1993	£650,000

DIVISION ONE RUNNERS-UP – 1975/1976

711.	15 pence
712.	Liverpool
713.	Everton
714.	Phil Parkes and Don Masson
715.	13
716.	True: losing away against Norwich City during April 1976
717.	24
718.	True: 2 wins and 3 draws
719.	Liverpool
720.	Gerry Francis

MIKE KEEN

721.	York City
722.	393
723.	Wing half
724.	Watford
725.	False: he owned two sports shops
726.	Luton Town
727.	39
728.	Thomas
729.	Wycombe Wanderers

730.   True

LEGENDS - 1
731.   Tony Ingham
732.   George Goddard
733.   Kevin Gallen
734.   John Gregory
735.   Ian Holloway
736.   Andy Sinton
737.   Phil Parkes
738.   Terry Fenwick
739.   Gareth Ainsworth
740.   Terry Venables

LEAGUE APPEARANCES
741.   David Bardsley   253
742.   Karl Ready   226
743.   Conway Smith   174
744.   Gareth Ainsworth   141
745.   Marcus Bignot   182
746.   Clarke Carlisle   96
747.   Trevor Francis   32
748.   Terrell Forbes   114
749.   Frank Clarke   67
750.   Peter Reid   29

PLAYING AWAY
751.   Stoke City
752.   Coventry City
753.   Bristol City
754.   Swansea City
755.   Doncaster Rovers

111

756.   *Oldham Athletic*

757.   *Tranmere Rovers*

758.   *Scunthorpe United*

759.   *Leicester City*

760.   *Sheffield United*

BRIAN BEDFORD

761.   *True*

762.   *Reading*

763.   *258*

764.   *Swindon Town*

765.   *AFC Bournemouth*

766.   *Brentford*

767.   *161*

768.   *Centre forward*

769.   *Welsh*

770.   *Scunthorpe United*

LEGENDS - 2

771.   *Rodney Marsh*

772.   *Dave Thomas*

773.   *Gerry Francis*

774.   *David Seaman*

775.   *Ray Wilkins*

776.   *Alan McDonald*

777.   *Paul Parker*

778.   *Les Ferdinand*

779.   *Stan Bowles*

780.   *Trevor Sinclair*

LEAGUE GOALSCORERS

781.   *Gary Bannister*   **56**

782.	Terry Mancini	3
783.	Simon Stainrod	48
784.	Terry Venables	19
785.	George Petchey	22
786.	Trevor Sinclair	16
787.	John Byrne	30
788.	Tony Sealy	18
789.	Dave Thomas	28
790.	Ernie Shepherd	51

FA CUP RUNNERS-UP - 1982

791.	West Bromwich Albion
792.	1-0 to Tottenham
793.	Terry Fenwick
794.	Peter Hucker
795.	Terry Venables
796.	False: it was only 5 days (final on 22 May and replay on 27 May)
797.	Crystal Palace
798.	Gary Waddock (Irish)
799.	Tony Currie
800.	5-1

NOTES

NOTES

OTHER BOOKS BY CHRIS COWLIN:

* Celebrities' Favourite Football Teams

* The British TV Sitcom Quiz Book

* The Cricket Quiz Book

* The Gooners Quiz Book

* The Horror Film Quiz Book

* The Official Aston Villa Quiz Book

* The Official Birmingham City Quiz Book

* The Official Brentford Quiz Book

* The Official Bristol Rovers Quiz Book

* The Official Burnley Quiz Book

* The Official Bury Quiz Book

* The Official Carlisle United Quiz Book

* The Official Carry On Quiz Book

* The Official Chesterfield Football Club Quiz Book

* The Official Colchester United Quiz Book

* The Official Coventry City Quiz Book

* The Official Doncaster Rovers Quiz Book

* The Official Greenock Morton Quiz Book

* The Official Heart of Midlothian Quiz Book

* The Official Hereford United Quiz Book

* The Official Hull City Quiz Book

* The Official Ipswich Town Quiz Book

* The Official Leicester City Quiz Book

OTHER BOOKS BY CHRIS COWLIN:

* The Official Macclesfield Town Quiz Book

* The Official Norwich City Football Club Quiz

* The Official Notts County Quiz Book

* The Official Peterborough United Quiz Book

* The Official Port Vale Quiz Book

* The Official Queen of the South Quiz Book

* The Official Queens Park Rangers Football Club Quiz Book

* The Official Rochdale AFC Quiz Book

* The Official Rotherham United Quiz Book

* The Official Sheffield United Quiz Book

* The Official Shrewsbury Town Quiz Book

* The Official Stockport County Quiz Book

* The Official Walsall Football Club Quiz Book

* The Official Watford Football Club Quiz Book

* The Official West Bromwich Albion Quiz Book

* The Official Wolves Quiz Book

* The Official Yeovil Town Quiz Book

* The Reality Television Quiz Book

* The Southend United Quiz Book

* The Spurs Quiz Book

* The Sunderland AFC Quiz Book

* The Ultimate Derby County Quiz Book

* The West Ham United Quiz Book

www.apexpublishing.co.uk